ONE-POT HEALTHY

ONE-POT HEALTHY

SABRINA FAUDA-RÔLE
PHOTOGRAPHY BY AKIKO IDA

Hardie Grant

BOOKS

CONTENTS

HEALTHY INGREDIENTS

UNPEELED VEGETABLES
WHENEVER POSSIBLE

LEAN MEATS: SKINLESS
CHICKEN, TURKEY,
RABBIT, VEAL ESCALOPE
OR RUMP STEAK, PORK
FILLET, 5% FAT MINCE,
OR PLANT-BASED
PROTEINS

LOW-FAT DAIRY
PRODUCTS OR
PLANT-BASED
CREAMS

STARCHY FOODS AND
GRAINS (PREFERABLY
WHOLEGRAIN)

DRIED HERBS AND SPICES,
STOCK CUBES, SOY SAUCE,
MISO, FRESH HERBS

JUST ONE POT?

A one-pot healthy dish is a complete dish which is low in calories but still packs in plenty of flavour. With everything cooked in a single pan, these classic or original recipes are quick and easy to prepare and perfect for the whole family.

The recipes in this book serve two to six people. They can be cooked on a suitable electric, gas or induction hob. You will need a steamer basket for some of the recipes.

Shopping is easy as most of the ingredients used in the recipes are available in supermarkets or wholefood shops. A few more unusual ingredients can be found in specialist shops or bought online. To make a one-pot healthy dish, you will need vegetables, lean proteins, some starchy foods, spices and low-fat dairy products.

Tips for successful one-pot healthy dishes:
– choose fruits and vegetables that are fresh and in season, and preferably organic if
  you are going to use the skins;
– choose meats from sources with higher welfare standards whenever possible;
– before you start, assemble all the ingredients and wash, then weigh and peel
  where necessary.

Almost all the recipes are complete meals, but you can also serve them with a side dish of green salad or lightly seasoned raw vegetables.

PUTTING TOGETHER A ONE-POT HEALTHY DISH

1.

CHOOSE VEGETABLES THAT ARE IN SEASON and if possible organically or sustainably grown. Where possible, do not peel vegetables so as to preserve their vitamins. You can also use frozen vegetables. Two-thirds of the dish can be made up of vegetables.

2.

ADD PLANT-BASED PROTEINS (pulses or tofu) or animal proteins (lean meat, fish or egg whites).

3.

ADD NATURAL AND HEALTHY FLAVOUR ENHANCERS SUCH AS ground or whole spices, onion, garlic, lemon zest, miso, soy sauce and stock cubes. Spices have natural digestive and anti-inflammatory properties.

4.

IF THE RECIPE CONTAINS DRY STARCHY FOODS, use higher-fibre ingredients if possible (wholewheat pasta, brown rice) or a variety of grains (spelt, buckwheat, for example).

5.

ADD A LOW-FAT DAIRY PRODUCT or plant-based cream made from soya, spelt or coconut, and so on.

6.

FATS AND OILS should be avoided or used in very small quantities. One spoonful is enough. Always choose plant-based products.

7.

ADD WATER if the recipe calls for it. For recipes based mainly on vegetables, very little water is needed as the vegetables will cook in their own steam as they release water.

8.

COOK FOR THE SPECIFIED TIME if the recipe tells you to, stir during cooking. Otherwise leave to cook without disturbing the mixture.

9.

SERVE with well-rinsed fresh herbs, lemon juice, soy sauce or chilli to add even more flavour, freshness and zing to your dish.

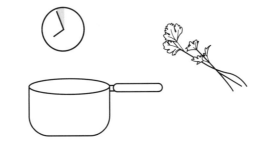

ESSENTIAL COOKING EQUIPMENT

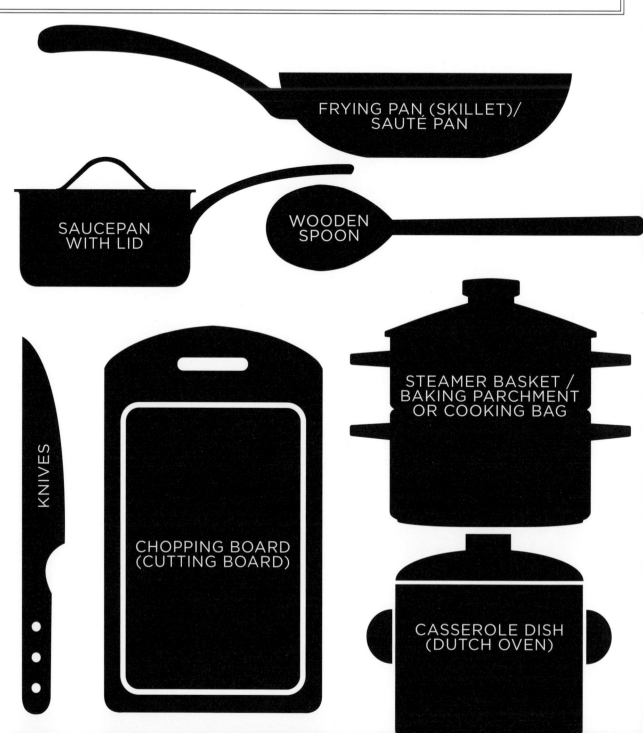

FRYING PAN (SKILLET)/
SAUTÉ PAN

SAUCEPAN
WITH LID

WOODEN
SPOON

STEAMER BASKET /
BAKING PARCHMENT
OR COOKING BAG

KNIVES

CHOPPING BOARD
(CUTTING BOARD)

CASSEROLE DISH
(DUTCH OVEN)

COOKING TIPS

VEGETABLE SPIRALS

- Special utensils such as spiralisers are available for making vegetable spirals or spaghetti.
- You can also use a vegetable peeler to cut strips of vegetables such as carrots, courgettes (zucchini) or parsnips.
- For larger vegetables, fine slices can be obtained with a mandolin.
- To cut a leek into long fine strips, cut off the dark green leaves at the top but leave the base intact. Hold the leek by the base. Insert the tip of a knife just under the base and cut the leek along its entire length. Repeat until the strips are suitably fine. Rinse the leek in a large bowl of water and cut off the base.

BAKING PARCHMENT PARCELS

To make the parcels, use large sheets of baking parchment and seal them tightly by folding them over several times or use some kitchen string. Cooking bags for use in the oven are also available and can be adapted to steam cooking. This practical solution is sealed with the clip provided.

PASTA, RICE & GRAINS

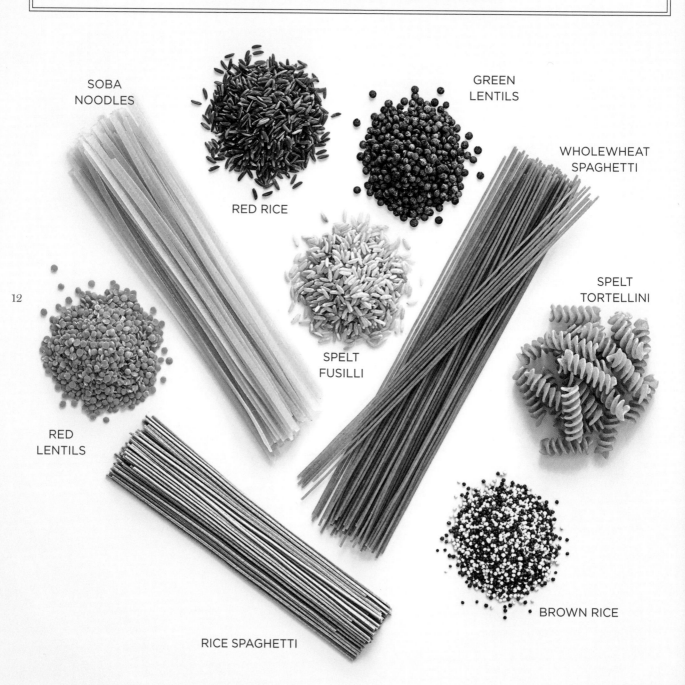

SOBA
NOODLES

RED RICE

GREEN
LENTILS

WHOLEWHEAT
SPAGHETTI

SPELT
FUSILLI

SPELT
TORTELLINI

12

RED
LENTILS

RICE SPAGHETTI

BROWN RICE

CREAMY INGREDIENTS

SOYA-BASED
CREAM

LOW-FAT
YOGHURT

LOW-FAT DOUBLE
(HEAVY) CREAM

SILKEN TOFU

PLANT-BASED DRINK

LOW-FAT SINGLE
(LIGHT) CREAM

STRONG FLAVOURS

MISO

DASHI BROTH

PARSLEY

GARLIC

THYME AND
BAY LEAF

CURRY
POWDER

OLIVES

SOY SAUCE

MUSHROOMS

14

CLOVES

CUMIN

HARISSA

CARDAMOM

GINGER

ONIONS

STOCK CUBE

LEAN ANIMAL PROTEINS

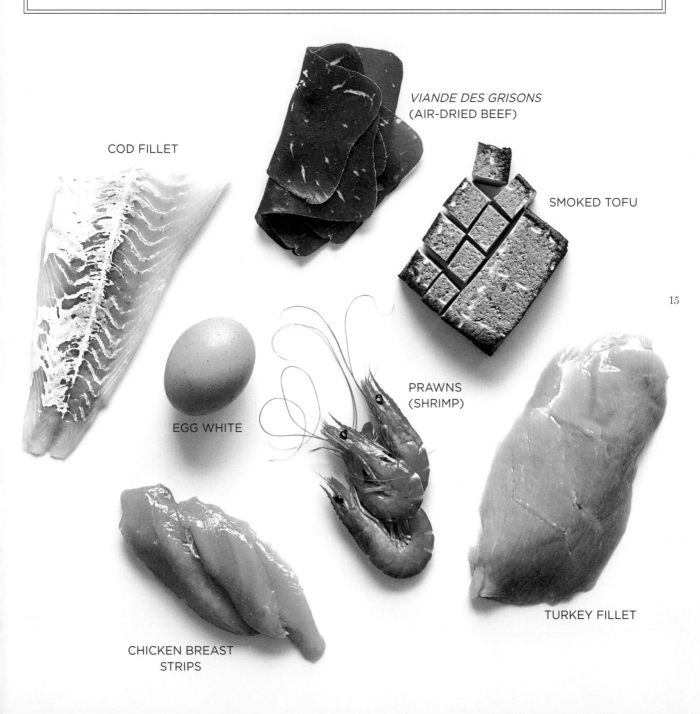

COD FILLET

VIANDE DES GRISONS
(AIR-DRIED BEEF)

SMOKED TOFU

EGG WHITE

PRAWNS
(SHRIMP)

TURKEY FILLET

CHICKEN BREAST
STRIPS

SUPER VEG

Simmered and sautéed, fat-free vegetarian recipes, cooked
quickly and simply to preserve vitamins and minerals.

PAN-FRIED PEPPERS AND SWEETCORN WITH GOAT'S CHEESE

Preparation: 5 minutes
Cooking time: 20 minutes

Serves 6

1 tablespoon olive oil
750 g (1 lb 10 oz) red, green and
    yellow (bell) peppers, cut into strips
400 g (14 oz) tin of sweetcorn
    (whole kernel corn), drained
1 red onion, thinly sliced
1 pinch of salt
100 g (3½ oz) soft goat's cheese
2 sprigs of mint, snipped
freshly ground black pepper

30 cm (12 in) frying pan (skillet)

method

Put the oil, peppers, sweetcorn, onion, salt and pepper in the frying pan. Cook over a medium heat for 20 minutes, stirring regularly. Add the goat's cheese and snipped mint. Mix, then serve.

SWEET AND SPICY CAULIFLOWER

Preparation: 10 minutes
Cooking time: 20 minutes

Serves 4

1 kg (2 lb 4 oz) cauliflower, cut into florets
1 tablespoon honey
1 teaspoon paprika
1 teaspoon ground cinnamon
1 teaspoon ground cumin
1 pinch of chilli powder

2 garlic cloves, chopped
1 pinch of salt
1 tablespoon olive oil
Choice of fresh herbs, to serve

26 cm (10 in) casserole dish (Dutch oven)

method

Put all the ingredients in the casserole dish. Cook over a high heat for
5 minutes, stirring regularly, then reduce the heat to low. Cover and simmer
for 15 minutes. Serve with snipped fresh herbs.

WINTER CASSEROLE

Preparation: 10 minutes
Cooking time: 20 minutes

22

Serves 4

300 g (10½ oz) celeriac (celery root), peeled and cut
   into 3 cm (1¼ in) cubes
2 leeks, cut into 2 cm (¾ in) sections
2 apples, peeled, cored and quartered
600 g (1 lb 5 oz) butternut squash, peeled, deseeded
   and cut into 3 cm (1¼ in) cubes
2 bay leaves

4 garlic cloves
1 pinch of salt
200 ml (7 fl oz/scant 1 cup) water
freshly ground black pepper

26 cm (10 in) casserole dish

method

Put all the ingredients in the casserole dish, cover and cook
over a low heat for 20 minutes. Serve immediately.

AUTUMN CASSEROLE

Preparation: 10 minutes
Cooking time: 20 minutes

Serves 4

250 g (9 oz) vacuum-packed or tinned chestnuts
300 g (10½ oz) green cabbage, cut into 2 cm (¾ in) slices
750 g (1 lb 10 oz) spinach, rinsed
2 carrots, cut into 1 cm (½ in) rounds

1 onion, thinly sliced
1 pinch of salt
200 ml (7 fl oz/scant 1 cup) water
freshly ground black pepper

26 cm (10 in) casserole dish (Dutch oven)

method

Put all the ingredients in the casserole dish, cover and cook
over a low heat for 20 minutes. Serve immediately.

SPRING CASSEROLE

Preparation: 10 minutes
Cooking time: 15 minutes

Serves 4

200 g (7 oz) fresh or frozen peas
1 large artichoke, cut into 8 (choke removed)
250g (9 oz) asparagus, cut into 5 cm (2 in) sections
300 g (10½ oz) new-season turnips, quartered
1 spring onion (scallion), thinly sliced

8 basil leaves
2 pinches of salt
200 ml (7 fl oz/scant 1 cup) water
freshly ground black pepper

24 cm (9½ in) saucepan

method

Put all the ingredients in the saucepan, cover and cook
over a low heat for 15 minutes. Serve immediately.

SUMMER CASSEROLE

Preparation: 10 minutes
Cooking time: 20 minutes

Serves 4

300 g (10½ oz) French (green) beans, topped and
    tailed
1 yellow (bell) pepper, thinly sliced
1 red (bell) pepper, thinly sliced
4 spring onions (scallions), halved lengthways
2 courgettes (zucchini), cut into fine strips

1 vegetable stock cube
6 basil leaves
4 sprigs of dill
4 sprigs of parsley
200 ml (7 fl oz/scant 1 cup) water

26 cm (10 in) casserole dish (Dutch oven)

method

Put all the ingredients in the casserole dish, cover and cook
over a low heat for 20 minutes. Serve immediately.

MEDITERRANEAN VEGETABLE CASSEROLE

Preparation: 10 minutes
Cooking time: 20 minutes

Serves 2

1 red (bell) pepper, cut into strips
3 tomatoes, cut into fine rounds
1 aubergine (eggplant), cut into thin slices
1 courgette (zucchini), cut into fine strips
150 ml (5 fl oz/scant ⅔ cup) water
2 tablespoons soy sauce
1 tablespoon olive oil
30 g (1 oz) olives, pitted and cut into rounds

4 sprigs of thyme
3 bay leaves
2 garlic cloves, thinly sliced
1 pinch of salt
freshly ground black pepper

26 cm (10 in) casserole dish (Dutch oven)

method

Arrange all the vegetables at the bottom of the casserole dish. Pour over
the water, soy sauce and olive oil. Add the olive slices, thyme, bay leaves,
garlic, salt and pepper. Cover and cook over a medium heat for 20 minutes.
The aubergines should be tender. Serve hot.

AUBERGINE CASSEROLE WITH FIGS

Preparation: 5 minutes
Cooking time: 20 minutes

32

Serves 6

150 ml (5 fl oz/scant ⅔ cup) water
1 tablespoon tomato purée (paste)
800 g (1 lb 12 oz) aubergines (eggplant), cut into
    5 mm (¼ in) strips
1 teaspoon cumin seeds
1 teaspoon ground cinnamon

2 figs, quartered
1 teaspoon oregano
12 basil leaves
1 pinch of salt
freshly ground black pepper

26 cm (10 in) saucepan

method

Mix the water and tomato purée together. Put all the ingredients in the saucepan and cook over a low heat for 20 minutes. Serve immediately.

AUTUMN TAGLIATELLE

Preparation: 15 minutes
Cooking time: 20 minutes

34

Serves 4

300 g (10½ oz) carrots, cut into tagliatelle
300 g (10½ oz) parsnips, cut into tagliatelle
300g (10½ oz) butternut squash, peeled and
    cut into tagliatelle
1 shallot, thinly sliced
1 teaspoon honey

1 tablespoon soy sauce
1 teaspoon dried oregano
1 pinch of salt
150 ml (5 fl oz/scant ⅔ cup) water
freshly ground black pepper

30 cm (12 in) frying pan (skillet)

method

Put all the ingredients in the frying pan, cover and cook over a medium heat
for about 20 minutes. Serve hot or warm.

VEGETABLE BOLOGNESE

Preparation: 10 minutes
Cooking time: 30 minutes

Serves 4

2 carrots, cut into fine strips
2 parsnips, cut into fine strips
400 g (14 oz) tin of chopped tomatoes
1 garlic clove, thinly sliced
1 onion, thinly sliced
100 g (3½ oz) red lentils
2 bay leaves

4 sprigs of thyme
1 tablespoon olive oil
1 pinch of salt
freshly ground black pepper
500 ml (17 fl oz/2 cups) water

26 cm (10 in) casserole dish (Dutch oven)

method

Put all the ingredients in the casserole dish and cook over a medium heat
for about 30 minutes, stirring regularly. Serve immediately.

CAULIFLOWER AND SOYA CASSEROLE

Preparation: 5 minutes
Cooking time: 20 minutes

38

Serves 4

500 g (1 lb 2 oz) cauliflower, cut into florets
200 ml (7 fl oz/scant 1 cup) soya-based cream
1 onion, thinly sliced
2 tablespoons soy sauce
1 garlic clove, chopped
1 pinch of salt
freshly ground black pepper

24 cm (9½ in) saucepan

method

Put all the ingredients in the saucepan, cover and cook over a medium heat
for about 20 minutes, mixing regularly. Serve immediately.

SOUPS & BROTHS

From a detox to a full meal, quick and easy one-pot
cooking for a comforting soup or broth.

MUSHROOM AND CHESTNUT VELOUTÉ SOUP

Preparation: 5 minutes
Cooking time: 30 minutes

Serves 4

500 g (1 lb 2 oz) closed-cup mushrooms
200 g (7 oz) tinned or vacuum-packed chestnuts
1 vegetable stock cube
1 onion, thinly sliced
500 ml (17 fl oz/2 cups) hazelnut milk
400 ml (13 fl oz/generous 1½ cups) water

1 pinch of salt
4 sprigs of parsley, leaves picked
Low-fat single (light) cream, to serve
freshly ground black pepper

26 cm (10 in) casserole dish (Dutch oven)

method

Put all the ingredients in the casserole dish and cook over a medium heat
for 30 minutes. Blend until smooth. Serve with freshly snipped parsley and
swirls of single cream.

SWISS CHARD AND VERMICELLI BROTH

Preparation: 5 minutes
Cooking time: 10 minutes

Serves 4

50 g (2 oz) vermicelli pasta
150 g (5 oz) Swiss chard, chopped
100 ml (3½ fl oz/scant ½ cup) concentrated
   dashi stock
1 tablespoon sesame oil
1 tablespoon sesame seeds
1 litre (34 fl oz/4 cups) water

26 cm (10 in) saucepan

method

Put all the ingredients in the saucepan. Bring to a boil and cook for
10 minutes, stirring occasionally. Serve hot.

CHICKEN AND VERMICELLI SOUP

Preparation: 5 minutes
Cooking time: 10 minutes

Serves 4

2 stock cubes
1 litre (34 fl oz/4 cups) water
250 g (9 oz) chicken breast fillets, sliced
50 g (2 oz) vermicelli pasta
500 g (1 lb 2 oz) carrots, grated
1 spring onion (scallion), thinly sliced
1 tablespoon soy sauce

26 cm (10 in) saucepan

method

Add the stock cubes to the water in the pan and bring to a boil. Add the rest of the ingredients and cook over a low heat for a further 5 minutes. Serve hot.

SPINACH VELOUTÉ SOUP

Preparation: 5 minutes
Cooking time: 15 minutes

Serves 4

500 g (1 lb 2 oz) fresh spinach, washed
1 onion, thinly sliced
2 vegetable stock cubes
100 g (3½ oz) low-fat cream cheese
400 ml (13 fl oz/generous 1½ cups) water

24 cm (9½ in) casserole dish (Dutch oven)

method

Put all the ingredients in the casserole dish and cook over a medium heat for
15 minutes. Blend until smooth. Serve hot.

SPINACH AND TOFU BROTH

Preparation: 10 minutes
Cooking time: 15 minutes

50

Serves 4

200 g (7 oz) spinach, rinsed and coarsely chopped
200 g (7 oz) tofu, diced
120 g (4 oz) miso
1 tablespoon sesame seeds
1 litre (34 fl oz/4 cups) water
Snipped chives, to serve

24 cm (9½ in) saucepan

method

Put all the ingredients except for the chives in the saucepan. Bring to a boil
and cook for 10 minutes, stirring occasionally. Serve hot with snipped chives.

BUTTERNUT SQUASH AND CHICKEN BROTH

Preparation: 10 minutes
Cooking time: 20 minutes

Serves 4

750 g (1 lb 10 oz) butternut squash, cut into
  spirals, or spaghetti
150 g (5 oz) chicken breast fillets, thinly sliced
1 leek, cut into fine strips
2 sprigs of rosemary
1 vegetable stock cube

7 level tablespoons low-fat double
  (heavy) cream
1 pinch of salt
1.5 litres (51 fl oz/6⅓ cups) water

26 cm (10 in) casserole dish (Dutch oven)

53

method

Put all the ingredients in the casserole dish and cook over a medium heat for 20 minutes. Serve immediately.

MONKFISH BROTH

Preparation: 5 minutes
Cooking time: 15 minutes   Resting time: 15 minutes

54

Serves 4

400 g (14 oz) monkfish, cut into 2–3 cm (¾–1¼ in)
   pieces
½ lemongrass stalk, cut in half lengthways
20 g (¾ oz) ginger, cut into 5 mm (¼ in) slices
1 pinch of chilli powder
1 spring onion (scallion), thinly sliced
juice and zest of 1 lime

1 teaspoon grated fresh turmeric or 1 pinch of
   ground turmeric
1 small bunch of coriander (cilantro), rinsed
1 pinch of salt
1.5 litres (51 fl oz/6⅓ cups) water

24 cm (9½ in) saucepan

method

Put all the ingredients except for the monkfish and the green of the onion in the saucepan. Boil over a medium heat for 15 minutes. Remove from the heat, immerse the pieces of monkfish, cover and leave to stand for 15 minutes. Sprinkle with the thinly sliced green part of the spring onion and serve.

COURGETTE AND TOFU VELOUTÉ SOUP

Preparation: 5 minutes
Cooking time: 10 minutes

56

Serves 4

600 g (1 lb 5 oz) courgettes (zucchini), cut into
 2 cm (¾ in) rounds
200 g (7 oz) silken tofu
1 onion, thinly sliced
12 mint leaves

1 garlic clove, chopped
1 vegetable stock cube
500 ml (17 fl oz/2 cups) water
freshly ground black pepper

24 cm (9½ in) saucepan

method

Put all the ingredients in the saucepan and cook over a medium heat for
10 minutes. Blend until smooth. Serve hot.

ASPARAGUS VELOUTÉ SOUP

Preparation: 5 minutes
Cooking time: 15 minutes

58

Serves 4

500 g (1 lb 2 oz) asparagus
750 ml (25 fl oz/3 cups) almond milk
1 onion, thinly sliced
2 sprigs of mint, leaves picked
2 celery stalks, leaves picked and stalks chopped
1 vegetable stock cube

24 cm (9½ in) saucepan

method

Cut off the tough bottom part of the asparagus. Put all the ingredients in the saucepan and cook over a medium heat for 15 minutes. Blend until smooth. Serve with freshly snipped mint.

HERB BROTH

Preparation: 10 minutes
Cooking time: 1 hour

60

Serves 4

1 bunch of coriander (cilantro)
1 bunch of parsley
1 bunch of chives
4 celery stalks, thinly sliced
2 bay leaves
1 onion, thinly sliced
2 garlic cloves, crushed

2 turnips, cut into 5 mm (¼ in) rounds
1 teaspoon peppercorns
1 teaspoon coriander seeds, crushed
2 pinches of salt
2 litres (70 fl oz/8 cups) water

26 cm (10 in) casserole dish (Dutch oven)

method

Put all the ingredients in the casserole dish, keeping a few chives aside.
Bring to a boil and cook over a low heat for 1 hour. Strain the broth and
serve hot with snipped fresh chives.

RAVIOLI BROTH

Preparation: 10 minutes
Cooking time: 30 minutes

62

Serves 4

120 g (4 oz) cheese and herb ravioli
1 carrot, cut into fine rounds
1 leek, thinly sliced
1 celery stalk, thinly sliced
1 bay leaf
1 garlic clove, chopped

3 cloves
4 cardamom pods, crushed
1 litre (34 fl oz/4 cups) water
1 pinch of salt

24 cm (9½ in) saucepan

method

Put the ravioli in the freezer. Put all the ingredients except for the ravioli in the saucepan. Bring to a boil and cook over a low heat for 30 minutes. Remove the ravioli from the freezer and immerse in the broth. Cook for the time stated on the packet and serve immediately.

KOMBU SEAWEED BROTH

Preparation: 5 minutes
Cooking time: 30 minutes   Resting time: 30 minutes

64

Serves 4

15 g (½ oz) kombu seaweed
10 g (½ oz) freshly grated ginger
200 g (7 oz) closed-cup mushrooms, quartered
1 spring onion (scallion), thinly sliced
1.5 litres (51 fl oz/6⅓ cups) water
1 pinch of salt

100 g (3½ oz) soba noodles
2 tablespoons soy sauce
50 g (2 oz) freshly grated black radish

24 cm (9½ in) saucepan

method

Put the kombu seaweed, ginger, mushrooms and white of the spring onion
in the saucepan with the water and salt. Cook over a very low heat for
20 minutes: the water should be just simmering. Remove from the heat, cover
and leave to stand for 30 minutes. Remove the kombu seaweed, bring to a
boil and add the soba noodles and soy sauce to the broth. Leave to cook for
10 minutes and serve hot, sprinkled with the grated black radish and thinly
sliced green part of the spring onion.

CHILLI BROTH

Preparation: 5 minutes
Cooking time: 20 minutes

66

Serves 4

½ fresh chilli
4 garlic cloves, crushed with skin left on
4 sun-dried tomatoes in oil, drained and chopped
2 shallots, thinly sliced
2 tablespoons red wine vinegar

1 teaspoon curry powder
200 g (7 oz) smoked tofu, diced
12 chives, snipped

24 cm (9½ in) saucepan

method

Put all the ingredients except for the chives in the saucepan. Bring to a boil and cook for 10 minutes, stirring occasionally. Serve hot with snipped chives.

ONION SOUP

Preparation: 5 minutes
Cooking time: 35 minutes

Serves 4

1 tablespoon olive oil
4 large onions, thinly sliced
4 tablespoons cornflour (cornstarch)
1.5 litres (51 fl oz/6⅓ cups) water
2 sprigs of thyme
1 garlic clove, chopped

1 pinch of salt
1 pinch of pepper
2 slices of toasted bread
4 sprigs of parsley, snipped

24 cm (9½ in) saucepan

method

Heat the olive oil in the saucepan, add the onions and cornflour. Cook for 5 minutes, stirring regularly. Add the water, thyme, garlic, salt and pepper and cook over a low heat for 30 minutes. Serve hot with the toasted bread cut into croutons and the snipped parsley.

STEAMED PARCEL DISHES

Recipes with ingredients that retain all their flavour
and vitamins thanks to a gentle cooking method
for healthy, easy, quick and tasty meals.

SCALLOP PARCEL

Preparation: 5 minutes
Cooking time: 10 minutes

Serves 2

500 g (1 lb 2 oz) asparagus
12 scallops
2 shallots, thinly sliced
100 ml (3½ fl oz/scant ½ cup) low-fat cream
8 chives, snipped

2 cardamom pods, crushed
1 pinch of ground Sichuan pepper
1 pinch of salt

26 cm (10 in) casserole dish (Dutch oven) + steamer basket

method

Cut off the tough bottom part of the asparagus, then cut in half lengthways. Put 500 ml (17 fl oz/2 cups) of water in the casserole dish and add the steamer basket. Place all the ingredients on a large sheet of baking parchment and fold over to make a parcel (or use a cooking bag). Put in the casserole dish. Cover, bring to a boil and cook over a low heat for 10 minutes. Open the parcel and serve immediately.

COD AND CELERIAC PARCEL

Preparation: 10 minutes
Cooking time: 10 minutes

Serves 4

500 g (1 lb 2 oz) cod fillets
500 g (1 lb 2 oz) celeriac (celery root), peeled
  and grated
2 leeks, cut into fine strips
100 ml (3½ fl oz/scant ½ cup) coconut milk

1 pinch of chilli powder
1 pinch of salt
½ lemongrass stalk, thinly sliced
freshly ground black pepper

26 cm (10 in) casserole dish (Dutch oven) + steamer
  basket

method

Put 500 ml (17 fl oz/2 cups) of water in the casserole dish and add the
steamer basket. Place all the ingredients on a large sheet of baking
parchment and fold over to make a parcel (or use a cooking bag). Put in the
casserole dish. Cover, bring to a boil and cook over a low heat for 10 minutes.
Open the parcel and serve immediately.

SALMON PARCEL

Preparation: 10 minutes
Cooking time: 10 minutes

76

Serves 4

2 salmon steaks
200 g (7 oz) frozen peas
4 slices of lemon
100 ml (3½ fl oz/scant ½ cup) plant-based cream
10 g (½ oz) ginger, cut into fine rounds
1 tablespoon soy sauce

4 sprigs of dill
1 pinch of salt
freshly ground black pepper

26 cm (10 in) casserole dish (Dutch oven) + steamer
  basket

method

Put 500 ml (17 fl oz/2 cups) of water in the casserole dish and add the steamer basket. Place all the ingredients on a large sheet of baking parchment and fold over to make a parcel (or use a cooking bag). Put in the casserole dish. Cover, bring to a boil and cook over a low heat for 10 minutes. Open the parcel and serve immediately.

SEA BASS PARCEL

Preparation: 10 minutes
Cooking time: 10 minutes

Serves 2

400 g (14 oz) sea bass fillet
1 courgette (zucchini), cut into fine strips
1 fennel bulb, thinly sliced
juice and zest of 1 orange
2 star anise
1 pinch of salt
freshly ground black pepper

26 cm (10 in) casserole dish (Dutch oven) + steamer
   basket

method

Put 500 ml (17 fl oz/2 cups) of water in the casserole dish and add the steamer basket. Place all the ingredients on a large sheet of baking parchment and fold over to make a parcel (or use a cooking bag). Put in the casserole dish. Cover, bring to a boil and cook over a low heat for 10 minutes. Open the parcel and serve immediately.

SKATE, TOMATO AND OLIVE PARCEL

Preparation: 5 minutes
Cooking time: 15 minutes

80

Serves 2

400 g (14 oz) skate fillet
40 g (1½ oz) black olives
250 g (9 oz) cherry tomatoes
1 courgette (zucchini), cut into fine strips
6 basil leaves
zest of ½ lemon
1 pinch of salt

26 cm (10 in) casserole dish (Dutch oven) + steamer
  basket

method

Put 500 ml (17 fl oz/2 cups) of water in the casserole dish and add the
steamer basket. Place all the ingredients on a large sheet of baking
parchment and fold over to make a parcel (or use a cooking bag). Put in the
casserole dish. Cover, bring to a boil and cook over a low heat for 15 minutes.
Open the parcel and serve immediately.

CHICKEN AND CELERIAC PARCEL

Preparation: 5 minutes
Cooking time: 15 minutes

82

Serves 4

2 chicken escalopes (about 300 g/10½ oz)
500 g (1 lb 2 oz) celeriac (celery root), peeled and
  cut into fine slices
100 g (3½ oz) cherry tomatoes
200 g (7 oz) fat-free quark

2 sprigs of thyme
1 pinch of salt
freshly ground black pepper

26 cm (10 in) casserole dish (Dutch oven) + steamer
  basket

method

Put 500 ml (17 fl oz/2 cups) of water in the casserole dish and add the
steamer basket. Place all the ingredients on a large sheet of baking
parchment and fold over to make a parcel (or use a cooking bag). Put in the
casserole dish. Cover, bring to a boil and cook over a low heat for 15 minutes.
Open the parcel and serve immediately.

TURKEY, LEEK AND COCONUT PARCEL

Preparation: 10 minutes
Cooking time: 20 minutes

84

Serves 4

2 turkey escalopes (about 300 g/10½ oz)
2 leeks, cut into fine strips
20 g (¾ oz) ginger, thinly sliced
1 tablespoon curry powder
200 ml (7 fl oz/scant 1 cup) coconut milk
6 sprigs of coriander (cilantro)
1 pinch of salt

26 cm (10 in) casserole dish (Dutch oven) + steamer
  basket

method

Put 500 ml (17 fl oz/2 cups) of water in the casserole dish and add the steamer basket. Place all the ingredients in a cooking bag (or use a large sheet of baking parchment and fold over to make a parcel). Put in the casserole dish. Cover, bring to a boil and cook over a low heat for 20 minutes. Open the parcel and serve immediately.

MACKEREL PARCEL

Preparation: 10 minutes
Cooking time: 15 minutes

86

Serves 4

4 large mackerel fillets
2 beetroot (beet), peeled and finely sliced
2 carrots, cut into fine strips
1 spring onion (scallion), thinly sliced
zest of ½ orange
2 sprigs of dill
1 teaspoon fennel seeds
1 pinch of salt

26 cm (10 in) casserole dish (Dutch oven) + steamer
   basket

method

Put 500 ml (17 fl oz/2 cups) of water in the casserole dish and add the steamer basket. Place all the ingredients on a large sheet of baking parchment and fold over to make a parcel (or use a cooking bag). Put in the casserole dish. Cover, bring to a boil and cook over a low heat for 15 minutes. Open the parcel and serve immediately.

KING PRAWN PARCEL

Preparation: 10 minutes
Cooking time: 10 minutes

88

Serves 2

12 king prawns (shrimp)
½ bunch of parsley
1 shallot, thinly sliced
6 slices of lemon
1 garlic clove, thinly sliced
300 g (10½ oz) mangetout (snow) peas
8 chives, snipped
1 tablespoon curry powder

26 cm (10 in) casserole dish (Dutch oven) + steamer
  basket

method

Put 500 ml (17 fl oz/2 cups) of water in the casserole dish and add the steamer basket. Place all the ingredients on a large sheet of baking parchment and fold over to make a parcel (or use a cooking bag). Put in the casserole dish. Cover, bring to a boil and cook over a low heat for 10 minutes. Open the parcel and serve immediately.

BROCCOLI AND TOFU PARCEL

Preparation: 5 minutes
Cooking time: 15 minutes

90

Serves 4

350 g (12 oz) broccoli, cut into florets
200 g (7 oz) smoked tofu, cut into 1 cm (½ in) slices
500 g (1 lb 2 oz) spinach, rinsed
2 tablespoons soy sauce
100 ml (3½ fl oz/scant ½ cup) soya-based cream
freshly ground black pepper

26 cm (10 in) casserole dish (Dutch oven) + steamer
  basket

method

Put 500 ml (17 fl oz/2 cups) of water in the casserole dish and add the steamer basket. Place all the ingredients on a large sheet of baking parchment and fold over to make a parcel (or use a cooking bag). Put in the casserole dish. Cover, bring to a boil and cook over a low heat for 15 minutes. Open the parcel and serve immediately.

STEAMED CARROT PARCEL

Preparation: 10 minutes
Cooking time: 15 minutes

Serves 4

1 organic orange
500 g (1 lb 2 oz) carrots, cut into fine strips
2 garlic cloves, chopped
1 tablespoon pistachios, chopped
1 tablespoon harissa
250 g (9 oz) low-fat yoghurt

50 g (2 oz) raisins
1 pinch of salt
4 sprigs of coriander (cilantro), leaves picked

26 cm (10 in) casserole dish (Dutch oven) + steamer
   basket

method

Zest half the orange, then squeeze it and collect the juice. Put 500 ml (17 fl oz/2 cups) of water in the casserole dish and add the steamer basket. Place all the ingredients on a large sheet of baking parchment and fold over to make a parcel (or use a cooking bag). Put in the casserole dish. Cover, bring to a boil and cook over a low heat for 15 minutes. Open the parcel, mix and serve immediately.

COLOURED CAULIFLOWER PARCEL

Preparation: 5 minutes
Cooking time: 15 minutes

94

Serves 4

500 g (1 lb 2 oz) romanesco cauliflower
300 g (10½ oz) cauliflower (white or a white and
   coloured mix)
2 tablespoons low-fat natural fromage frais
1 spring onion (scallion), thinly sliced

1 tablespoon curry powder
1 pinch of salt
freshly ground black pepper

26 cm (10 in) casserole dish (Dutch oven) + steamer
   basket

method

Put 500 ml (17 fl oz/2 cups) of water in the casserole dish and add the steamer basket. Place all the ingredients on a large sheet of baking parchment and fold over to make a parcel (or use a cooking bag). Put in the casserole dish. Cover, bring to a boil and cook over a low heat for 15 minutes. Open the parcel and serve immediately.

STEAMED FRENCH BEAN PARCEL

Preparation: 10 minutes
Cooking time: 15 minutes

Serves 4

30 g (1 oz) pine nuts
1 bunch of basil, leaves picked
1 tablespoon olive oil
1 garlic clove, chopped
1 pinch of salt
100 g (3½ oz/generous ½ cup) wholewheat couscous
500 g (1 lb 2 oz) French beans, topped and tailed

26 cm (10 in) casserole dish (Dutch oven) + steamer
  basket

method

Put 500 ml (17 fl oz/2 cups) of water in the casserole dish and add the steamer basket. Mix the pine nuts with the basil, olive oil, garlic and salt. Place the couscous, French beans and basil mixture on a large sheet of baking parchment, sprinkle with 2 tablespoons of water and fold over to make a parcel (or use a cooking bag). Put in the casserole dish. Cover, bring to a boil and cook over a low heat for 15 minutes. Open the parcel, mix and serve immediately.

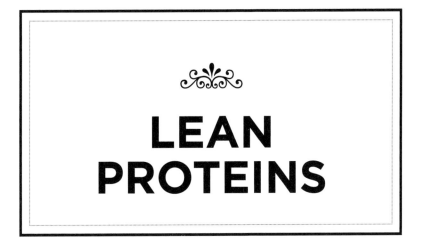

LEAN PROTEINS

Recipes based on low-fat protein and vegetables for complete and balanced meals. Suitable for athletes requiring protein-rich dishes.

TOMATO, OLIVE AND HERB OMELETTE

Preparation: 10 minutes
Cooking time: 5-6 minutes

Serves 6

6 egg whites
1 pinch of salt
2 tablespoons soft goat's cheese
1 garlic clove, chopped
1 pinch of Espelette pepper
1 bunch of mixed herbs (parsley, chives, chervil),
   snipped

1 tablespoon olive oil
250 g (9 oz) cherry tomatoes, halved
25 g (¾ oz) black olives, pitted and cut
   into rounds
freshly ground black pepper

30 cm (12 in) frying pan (skillet)

method

Beat the egg whites for 1 minute with the salt, pepper, 1 tablespoon of the goat's cheese, garlic, Espelette pepper and snipped herbs. Heat the frying pan over a medium heat, add the oil and the egg white mixture and sprinkle the tomatoes, olive rounds and pieces of goat's cheese on top.
Cook for 5 to 6 minutes. Serve hot.

VEGETABLE OMELETTE

Preparation: 10 minutes
Cooking time: 5–6 minutes

Serves 6

6 egg whites
1 pinch of salt
1 courgette (zucchini), cut into fine strips
1 carrot, cut into fine strips
1 tablespoon olive oil

12 basil leaves, snipped
1 spring onion (scallion), thinly sliced
freshly ground black pepper

30 cm (12 in) frying pan (skillet)

method

Beat the egg whites with the salt and pepper for 1 minute, add the courgette and carrot strips and mix together. Heat the oil in the frying pan over a medium heat, add the egg white mixture and sprinkle the snipped basil and thinly sliced onion on top. Cook for 5 to 6 minutes. Serve hot.

VIANDE DES GRISONS (AIR-DRIED BEEF) OMELETTE

Preparation: 10 minutes
Cooking time: 5–6 minutes

Serves 6

6 egg whites
1 pinch of salt
6 closed-cup mushrooms, thinly sliced
1 small white onion, thinly sliced
4 sprigs of dill, snipped

70 g (2¼ oz) Viande des Grisons (air-dried beef)
1 tablespoon olive oil
freshly ground black pepper

30 cm (12 in) frying pan (skillet)

method

Beat the egg whites with the salt and pepper for 1 minute. Add the
mushrooms, onion and dill and mix together. Cut the Viande des Grisons into
thin strips. Heat the oil in the frying pan over a medium heat, add the egg
white mixture and sprinkle with the Viande des Grisons.
Cook for 5 to 6 minutes. Serve immediately.

PAN-FRIED TURKEY WITH PEPPERS

Preparation: 5 minutes
Cooking time: 13 minutes

Serves 4

250 g (9 oz) turkey fillets, cut into thin strips
1 tablespoon ras el hanout
½ preserved lemon, chopped
1 green (bell) pepper, thinly sliced
1 yellow (bell) pepper, thinly sliced
1 red (bell) pepper, thinly sliced

1 red onion, thinly sliced
2 pinches of salt
4 sprigs of coriander (cilantro), leaves picked
freshly ground black pepper

24 cm (9½ in) sauté pan

method

Heat a non-stick sauté pan over a high heat. Brown the turkey
fillets with the ras el hanout for 3 minutes. Add all the other
ingredients except for the coriander. Fry for a further 10 minutes,
stirring. Serve sprinkled with coriander leaves.

CHICKEN WITH BUTTERNUT SQUASH AND PISTACHIOS

Preparation: 10 minutes
Cooking time: 25 minutes

Serves 4

1 tablespoon olive oil
1 onion, thinly sliced
1 tablespoon curry powder
250 g (9 oz) chicken breast, cut into thin strips
1 garlic clove, chopped
400 g (14 oz) butternut squash, peeled and diced
200 ml (7 fl oz/scant 1 cup) low-fat cream

1 tablespoon pistachios, shelled
  and chopped
150 ml (5 fl oz/scant ⅔ cup) apple juice
1 pinch of salt
freshly ground black pepper

30 cm (12 in) sauté pan

method

Heat the oil in the sauté pan over a medium heat. Add the onion, curry powder, chicken and chopped garlic. Fry for 5 minutes, stirring regularly. Add the rest of the ingredients, mix together, cover and cook for about 20 minutes. Serve immediately.

TURKEY WITH SWEET POTATOES AND SPICES

Preparation: 10 minutes
Cooking time: 20 minutes

Serves 4

1 tablespoon olive oil
1 onion, thinly sliced
200 g (7 oz) turkey escalopes, cut into thin strips
800 g (1 lb 12 oz) sweet potatoes, cut into pieces
1 pinch of nutmeg
1 cinnamon stick

1 pinch of paprika
200 ml (7 fl oz/scant 1 cup) water
1 pinch of salt
freshly ground black pepper

24 cm (9½ in) saucepan

method

Heat the oil in the pan, add the onion and strips of turkey and cook
for 5 minutes, stirring. Add the rest of the ingredients, cover and cook
for 15 minutes. Serve immediately.

MACKEREL CASSEROLE

Preparation: 5 minutes
Cooking time: 15 minutes   Resting time: 15 minutes

112

Serves 4

4 onions, thinly sliced
1 carrot, cut into fine rounds
2 sprigs of thyme
2 bay leaves
8 sprigs of parsley
1 teaspoon coarse salt
200 ml (7 fl oz/scant 1 cup) white wine

4 whole mackerel, gutted
1 teaspoon coriander seeds, crushed
1 teaspoon white peppercorns
1 teaspoon fennel seeds

26 cm (10 in) casserole dish
   (Dutch oven)

method

Put the onions, carrot, thyme, bay leaf and parsley in the bottom of the casserole dish. Add the salt and white wine, lay the mackerel on top and sprinkle with the spices. Cover and cook over a medium heat for 15 minutes. Remove from the heat and leave to stand for 15 minutes before serving.

CHICKEN, POTIMARRON SQUASH AND DATE CASSEROLE

Preparation: 5 minutes
Cooking time: 20 minutes

Serves 6

300 g (10½ oz) chicken breast fillets, cut into thin strips
8 dates
1 kg (2 lb 4 oz) potimarron squash, deseeded and cut into 1 cm (½ in) slices
1 tablespoon coriander seeds, crushed

10 g (½ oz) ginger, chopped
1 onion, thinly sliced
1 pinch of salt
250 ml (8½ fl oz/1 cup) water
freshly ground black pepper

26 cm (10 in) casserole dish (Dutch oven)

method

Put all the ingredients in the casserole dish. Cover and cook over a
low heat for 20 minutes. Serve immediately.

MUSSEL CASSEROLE

Preparation: 10 minutes
Cooking time: 10 minutes

Serves 4

1.2 litres (40 fl oz/4¾ cups) mussels
1 teaspoon salt
4 celery stalks, chopped
1 bunch of parsley, chopped
1 shallot, finely chopped

1 tablespoon aniseed
150 ml (5 fl oz/scant ⅔ cup) white wine
175 ml (6 fl oz/¾ cup) low-fat cream

26 cm (10 in) casserole dish (Dutch oven)

method

Put the mussels in the casserole dish with the salt, celery, parsley, shallot and aniseed. Cook over a medium heat for 2 minutes, stirring regularly.
Add the white wine, cover and cook for 5 to 10 minutes, stirring regularly.
Add the cream and toss the mussels before serving.

THAI COCKLE CASSEROLE

Preparation: 10 minutes
Cooking time: 7 minutes

118

Serves 4

1.2 litres (40 fl oz/4¾ cups) cockles
1 pinch of salt
½ bunch of parsley, chopped
½ bunch of coriander (cilantro), chopped
20 g (¾ oz) ginger, chopped
1 lemongrass stalk, chopped

2 spring onions (scallions), thinly sliced
150 ml (5 fl oz/scant ⅔ cup) water
2 tablespoons nuoc mam (Vietnamese fish sauce)
freshly ground black pepper

26 cm (10 in) casserole dish (Dutch oven)

method

Put the cockles in the casserole dish with the salt, pepper, parsley, coriander, ginger, lemongrass and spring onions. Cook over a medium heat for 2 minutes, stirring regularly. Add the water and nuoc mam sauce, cover and cook for 5 minutes, stirring regularly. Serve immediately.

CHICKEN, CABBAGE AND CARROT CASSEROLE

Preparation: 10 minutes
Cooking time: 15 minutes

Serves 4

300 g (10½ oz) chicken breast,
  cut into thin strips
500 g (1 lb 2 oz) white cabbage, shredded
250 g (9 oz) carrots, cut into thin strips
1 shallot, thinly sliced
1 tablespoon olive oil

1 tablespoon miso
1 pinch of salt
200 ml (7 fl oz/scant 1 cup) water
freshly ground black pepper

26 cm (10 in) casserole dish (Dutch oven)

method

Put all the ingredients in the casserole dish. Cover and cook over a medium
heat for 15 minutes, stirring regularly. Serve immediately.

RABBIT WITH CARROTS

Preparation: 5 minutes
Cooking time: 45 minutes

122

Serves 4

4 rabbit legs
250 g (9 oz) carrots, cut into 1 cm (½ in) rounds
1 onion, thinly sliced
2 star anise
500 ml (17 fl oz/2 cups) white wine
2 bay leaves

2 sprigs of thyme
4 juniper berries
1 teaspoon whole peppercorns
1 pinch of salt

30 cm (12 in) frying pan (skillet)

method

Put all the ingredients in the frying pan. Cover and cook over a low heat for
45 minutes. There should be no liquid left in the bottom of the pan.
Serve immediately.

PAN-FRIED CHICKEN LIVERS

Preparation: 5 minutes
Cooking time: 10 minutes

Serves 4

1 tablespoon olive oil
6 closed-cup mushrooms, thinly sliced
1 garlic clove, chopped
500 g (1 lb 2 oz) chicken livers
1 pinch of salt
2 tablespoons balsamic vinegar

2 sprigs of mint, snipped
4 sprigs of parsley, snipped
freshly ground black pepper

30 cm (12 in) frying pan (skillet)

method

Heat the olive oil in the frying pan, add the mushrooms and garlic.
Cook over a medium heat for 5 minutes, then add the chicken livers,
salt and pepper. Cook for a further 3 minutes over a high heat,
then add the balsamic vinegar. Cook for a further 2 minutes and
serve immediately sprinkled with chopped mint and parsley.

PORK TENDERLOIN WITH WHITE CHICORY

Preparation: 10 minutes
Cooking time: 30 minutes

Serves 4

1 tablespoon olive oil
500 g (1 lb 2 oz) pork tenderloin
2 shallots, thinly sliced
1 tablespoon honey
4 white chicory (endive), cut in 4 lengthways
1 cinnamon stick

200 ml (7 fl oz/scant 1 cup) low-fat cream
1 teaspoon peppercorns
1 pinch of salt

24 cm (9½ in) sauté pan

method

Heat the oil in the sauté pan, then brown the pork tenderloin on all sides for 3 to 4 minutes. Add the shallots and honey, then cook for a further 2 minutes, stirring. Add all the other ingredients and stir. Cover and cook over a low heat for 25 minutes. Serve immediately.

PAN-FRIED PRAWNS AND VEGETABLES

Preparation: 10 minutes
Cooking time: 7 minutes

128

Serves 4

1 tablespoon sesame oil
1 spring onion (scallion)
150 g (5 oz) mangetout (snow) peas
200 g (7 oz) red radishes, cut into fine rounds
1 courgette (zucchini), cut into fine rounds
2 teaspoons tandoori spices
500 g (1 lb 2 oz) cooked prawns (shrimp)

1 small pot fat-free yoghurt
1 garlic clove, chopped
1 pinch of salt
4 sprigs of mint, leaves picked and snipped

30 cm (12 in) frying pan (skillet)

method

Heat the sesame oil in the frying pan, add the vegetables with a teaspoon of
the tandoori spices and fry over a high heat for 5 minutes. Add the prawns
and fry for a further 2 minutes. Mix the yoghurt with the chopped garlic,
salt and remaining teaspoon of tandoori spices. Serve the vegetables and
prawns with the yoghurt sauce, sprinkled with chopped mint.

VEAL WITH PINEAPPLE

Preparation: 5 minutes
Cooking time: 20 minutes

Serves 6

400 g (14 oz) veal rump, cut into 3 cm (1¼ in) pieces
½ pineapple, cut into 3 cm (1¼ in) cubes
3 celery stalks, thinly sliced
1 red onion, thinly sliced
1 tablespoon olive oil

1 tablespoon curry powder
1 pinch of salt
freshly ground black pepper

26 cm (10 in) sauté pan

method

Put all the ingredients in the sauté pan. Cover and cook
over a medium heat for 20 minutes, stirring regularly. Serve hot.

SAUTÉED BEEF WITH PEAS

Preparation: 5 minutes
Cooking time: 10 minutes

132

Serves 4

350 g (12 oz) 5% fat minced (ground) beef
250 g (9 oz) frozen peas
1 tablespoon whole cumin seeds
1 onion, chopped
250 g (9 oz) cherry tomatoes, halved
2 sprigs of mint, leaves picked
2 sprigs of parsley, leaves picked

1 tablespoon olive oil
1 pinch of salt
freshly ground black pepper
zest of 1 lemon, to serve

30 cm (12 in) frying pan (skillet)

method

Put all the ingredients in the pan except for the lemon zest.
Cook over a high heat for 10 minutes, stirring regularly.
Serve hot with grated lemon zest.

PAN-FRIED FRESH TUNA AND VEGETABLES

Preparation: 10 minutes
Cooking time: 10 minutes

134

Serves 4

2 tablespoons sesame seeds
2 × 300 g (10½ oz) tuna steaks
1 tablespoon olive oil
20 g (¾ oz) freshly grated ginger
300 g (10½ oz) Chinese leaves (Napa cabbage),
   thinly sliced

1 green (bell) pepper, cut into matchsticks
2 courgettes (zucchini), cut into fine strips
2 tablespoons soy sauce
juice and zest of 1 lime

30 cm (12 in) frying pan (skillet)

method

Put the sesame seeds on a plate and coat the tuna steaks. Heat the oil in the frying pan, add the ginger, Chinese leaves, pepper and courgette strips. Cook over a medium heat for 5 minutes, stirring regularly, then add the soy sauce and stir. Move the vegetables to the side of the pan and add the tuna steaks. Leave to cook for 4 minutes without touching them. Turn the steaks, cook for a further minute and remove from the heat. Serve immediately, sprinkled with the lime juice and zest.

TURKEY WITH CREAM AND MUSHROOMS

Preparation: 10 minutes
Cooking time: 15 minutes

Serves 4

300 g (10½ oz) turkey fillets
200 g (7 oz) courgette (zucchini), cut into fine strips
250 g (9 oz) closed-cup mushrooms, quartered
1 tablespoon wholegrain mustard
1 shallot, thinly sliced
175 ml (6 fl oz/¾ cup) low-fat cream

1 pinch of salt
zest of 1 lemon
freshly ground black pepper

26 cm (10 in) saucepan

method

Put all the ingredients in the saucepan. Cook for 15 minutes,
stirring regularly. Serve immediately.

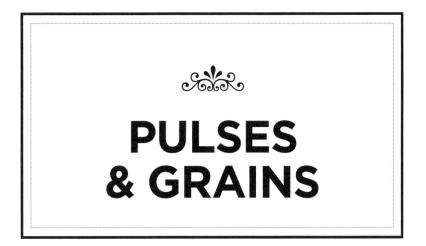

PULSES & GRAINS

Plant proteins and grains for generous and complete meals. Simple to make in record time with ingredients that ring the changes.

BURGHUL WITH COD AND COURGETTE

Preparation: 5 minutes
Cooking time: 10 minutes

140

Serves 4

200 g (7 oz/scant 1¼ cups) burghul
400 g (14 oz) courgette (zucchini), cut into fine strips
1 tablespoon tomato purée (paste)
1 garlic clove, thinly sliced
400 ml (13 fl oz/generous 1½ cups) water
400 g (14 oz) cod

1 pinch of salt
1 tablespoon oregano
zest of ½ lemon
freshly ground black pepper

30 cm (12 in) frying pan (skillet)

method

Put the burghul and courgettes in the bottom of the frying pan. Mix the burghul with the tomato purée, garlic and water. Place the cod on top, season with salt, pepper, oregano and lemon zest. Cover and cook over a medium heat for 10 minutes. Remove from the heat, keep covered and leave to stand for 10 minutes before serving.

BURGHUL WITH TOMATOES

Preparation: 5 minutes
Cooking time: 10 minutes

Serves 4

200 g (7 oz/scant 1¼ cups) burghul
20 g (¾ oz) sun-dried tomatoes in oil, drained
  and thinly sliced
4 celery stalks, thinly sliced
20 g (¾ oz) raisins
2 tomatoes, cut into rounds
1 teaspoon cumin seeds

1 teaspoon fennel seeds
1 pinch of salt
400 ml (13 fl oz/generous 1½ cups) water
freshly ground black pepper

24 cm (9½ in) saucepan

method

Put all the ingredients in the saucepan, cover and cook over a low heat
for 10 minutes. Serve immediately.

QUINOA, CARROTS AND PARSNIPS

Preparation: 15 minutes
Cooking time: 20 minutes

144

Serves 4

400 g (14 oz) tinned chickpeas (garbanzos)
300 g (10½ oz) carrots, peeled and cut into
 1 cm (½ in) rounds
300 g (10½ oz) parsnips, peeled and cut into
 1 cm (½ in) rounds
200 g (7 oz/1 cup) quinoa
4 sprigs of parsley, leaves picked
4 sprigs of coriander (cilantro), leaves picked

1 tablespoon olive oil
1 teaspoon ras el hanout
500 ml (17 fl oz/2 cups) water
1 pinch of salt
freshly ground black pepper

24 cm (9½ in) saucepan

method

Put all the ingredients in the saucepan and cook over a medium heat for
about 20 minutes, stirring regularly. Serve immediately with
some fresh herbs.

LENTILS WITH TOFU

Preparation: 10 minutes
Cooking time: 35 minutes

146

Serves 6

250 g (9 oz/1⅓ cups) green lentils
200 g (7 oz) smoked tofu, diced
1 red (bell) pepper, cut into 1 cm (½ in) pieces
250 g (9 oz) potatoes, diced
1 onion, thinly sliced
1 teaspoon cumin seeds
1 teaspoon oregano

4 sprigs of parsley, leaves picked
1 pinch of salt
freshly ground black pepper
750 ml (25 fl oz/3 cups) water

24 cm (9½ in) saucepan

method

Put all the ingredients in the saucepan and cook over a medium heat for
about 35 minutes, stirring regularly. Serve with a little snipped parsley.

CHICKPEA AND TOMATO CASSEROLE

Preparation: 10 minutes
Cooking time: 20 minutes

Serves 4

650 g (1 lb 7 oz) tinned chickpeas/garbanzos
   (450 g/1 lb drained weight)
500 g (1 lb 2 oz) tomato passata
1 onion, thinly sliced
100 g (3½ oz) carrots, cut into rounds
1 teaspoon ground turmeric
1 teaspoon fennel seeds
1 teaspoon paprika

2 sprigs of thyme
2 bay leaves
2 cloves
100 ml (3½ fl oz/scant ½ cup) water
1 pinch of salt
freshly ground black pepper

24 cm (9½ in) saucepan

method

Put all the ingredients in the saucepan. Cook over a medium heat for
20 minutes. Stir before serving immediately.

RED LENTIL DAHL

Preparation: 10 minutes
Cooking time: 30 minutes

150

Serves 6

250 g (9 oz/1 cup) red lentils
200 ml (7 fl oz/scant 1 cup) low-fat double
  (heavy) cream
1 garlic clove, thinly sliced
250 g (9 oz) carrots, cut into fine rounds
1 teaspoon cumin seeds
1 teaspoon ground turmeric

1 teaspoon ground coriander
1 pinch of chilli powder
1 pinch of salt
freshly ground black pepper
750 ml (25 fl oz/3 cups) water

24 cm (9½ in) saucepan

method

Put all the ingredients in the saucepan and cook over a medium heat for about 30 minutes, stirring regularly. Serve immediately.

LENTIL AND HADDOCK CASSEROLE

Preparation: 10 minutes
Cooking time: 30 minutes

152

Serves 4

200 g (7 oz/generous 1 cup)
  beluga lentils
500 g (1 lb 2 oz) tomatoes, sliced
1 onion, thinly sliced
2 celery stalks, thinly sliced
100 g (3½ oz) haddock, shredded
1 teaspoon coriander seeds, crushed
1 teaspoon cumin seeds
600 ml (20 fl oz/2½ cups) water
freshly ground black pepper

24 cm (9½ in) saucepan

method

Put all the ingredients in the saucepan. Cook over a medium heat for
30 minutes, stirring regularly. Serve hot.

QUINOA AND VEGETABLE CASSEROLE

Preparation: 10 minutes
Cooking time: 25 minutes

Serves 4

100 g (3½ oz/½ cup) quinoa, rinsed and drained
500 g (1 lb 2 oz) butternut squash, peeled and
   cut into 2 cm (¾ in) cubes
500 g (1 lb 2 oz) cauliflower, cut into florets
1 courgette (zucchini), cut into 1 cm (½ in) rounds
1 tablespoon harissa
1 onion, thinly sliced

1 vegetable stock cube
6 sprigs of parsley, leaves picked
1 pinch of salt
freshly ground black pepper
750 ml (25 fl oz/3 cups) water

26 cm (10 in) casserole dish (Dutch oven)

method

Put all the ingredients in the casserole dish. Cover and cook over a medium
heat for 25 minutes. Stir before serving hot.

RICE & PASTA

Quick and tasty, fat-free recipes based on
slow-release sugars for delightful meals.

RICE NOODLES WITH PRAWNS

Preparation: 5 minutes
Cooking time: 10 minutes

Serves 4

250 g (9 oz) rice noodles
350 g (12 oz) raw prawns (shrimp)
1 green chilli
2 tablespoons nuoc mam (Vietnamese fish sauce)
2 tablespoons grated coconut, plus extra to garnish

250 ml (8½ fl oz/1 cup) water
juice and zest of 1 lime
4 sprigs of basil

30 cm (12 in) frying pan (skillet)

159

method

Soak the rice noodles in plenty of cold water for 15 minutes. Heat the frying pan over a medium heat and add the prawns, chilli, nuoc mam and coconut. Cook for 3 minutes, then add the water and rice noodles. Cook for 7 minutes, stirring regularly. Serve with the lime juice and zest, sprinkled with chopped basil and grated coconut.

SPAGHETTI WITH TOMATOES

Preparation: 5 minutes
Cooking time: 15 minutes

Serves 4

250 g (9 oz) wholewheat spaghetti
500 g (1 lb 2 oz) cherry tomatoes, halved
20 basil leaves
1 onion, thinly sliced
1 teaspoon chilli purée (paste)
1 garlic clove, thinly sliced

1 teaspoon coarse salt
2 pinches of freshly ground black pepper
600 ml (20 fl oz/2½ cups) water

26 cm (10 in) casserole dish (Dutch oven)

method

Put all the ingredients in the casserole dish and cook over a medium heat for about 15 minutes, stirring regularly. Serve with freshly snipped basil.

RICE WITH VEAL AND MUSHROOMS

Preparation: 10 minutes
Cooking time: 25 minutes

162

Serves 4

1 tablespoon olive oil
400 g (14 oz) minced (ground) veal
1 shallot, thinly sliced
200 g (7 oz/scant 1 cup) white short-grain rice
500 g (1 lb 2 oz) mushrooms, halved
4 sprigs of thyme

1 teaspoon coarse salt
600 ml (20 fl oz/2½ cups) water
4 sprigs of parsley, snipped
freshly ground black pepper

26 cm (10 in) casserole dish (Dutch oven)

method

Heat the oil in the casserole dish over a medium heat. Add the veal and
shallot, brown for 3 minutes, then add the rice, mushrooms, thyme, salt and
pepper, followed by the water. Mix together and cook over a medium heat for
25 minutes. Serve with snipped parsley.

BROWN RICE WITH VEGETABLES

Preparation: 10 minutes
Cooking time: 45 minutes

Serves 4

250 g (9 oz/1¼ cups) brown rice
1 yellow (bell) pepper, thinly sliced
1 red (bell) pepper, thinly sliced
1 green (bell) pepper, thinly sliced
1 onion, thinly sliced
75 g (2½ oz) raisins
12 sprigs of coriander (cilantro), leaves picked

200 ml (7 fl oz/scant 1 cup) coconut milk
1 litre (34 fl oz/4 cups) water
1 teaspoon salt
freshly ground black pepper
Grated coconut, to serve

26 cm (10 in) saucepan

method

Put all the ingredients in the saucepan and cook over a low heat for
45 minutes. Serve with grated coconut and a little snipped coriander.

RED RICE WITH CALAMARI

Preparation: 10 minutes
Cooking time: 45 minutes

166

Serves 4

150 g (5 oz/generous ⅔ cup) red rice
500 g (1 lb 2 oz) calamari
400 g (14 oz) tinned chopped tomatoes
large pinch of saffron (0.2 g)
1 garlic clove, chopped
1 onion, thinly sliced
1 carrot, cut into rounds

6 sprigs of parsley, leaves picked
750 ml (25 fl oz/3 cups) water
1 teaspoon salt
freshly ground black pepper

26 cm (10 in) casserole dish (Dutch oven)

method

Put all the ingredients in the casserole dish and cook over a low heat for
45 minutes. Serve with freshly snipped parsley.

FUSILLI PASTA WITH MUSHROOMS

Preparation: 10 minutes
Cooking time: 15 minutes

Serves 4

200 g (7 oz) spelt fusilli
1 shallot, thinly sliced
500 g (1 lb 2 oz) closed-cup
    mushrooms, halved
12 sage leaves
350 g (12 oz) low-fat quark
1 teaspoon coarse salt
500 ml (17 fl oz/2 cups) water
freshly ground black pepper

26 cm (10 in) saucepan

method

Put all the ingredients in the saucepan and cook over a medium heat for
about 15 minutes, stirring regularly. Serve immediately.

MUSHROOM RISOTTO

Preparation: 10 minutes
Cooking time: 25 minutes

Serves 6

250 g (9 oz/scant 1¼ cups) risotto rice
 (carnaroli, arborio, etc.)
1 shallot, thinly sliced
400 g (14 oz) shiitake or closed-cup mushrooms,
 quartered
10 g (½ oz) dried morel mushrooms

100 ml (3½ fl oz/scant ½ cup) low-fat single (light)
 cream
2 sprigs of thyme
250 ml (8½ fl oz/1 cup) white wine
1 stock cube
650 ml (22 fl oz/2¾ cups) water
freshly ground black pepper

24 cm (9½ in) sauté pan

method

Put all the ingredients in the sauté pan and cook over a medium heat for
about 25 minutes, stirring regularly. Serve immediately.

VEGETABLE RISOTTO

Preparation: 10 minutes
Cooking time: 25 minutes

Serves 6

250 g (9 oz/scant 1¼ cups) risotto rice (carnaroli,
   arborio, etc.)
1 courgette (zucchini), diced
1 yellow (bell) pepper, diced
125 g (4 oz) frozen peas
1 shallot, thinly sliced

250 ml (8½ fl oz/1 cup) white wine
1 stock cube
750 ml (25 fl oz/3 cups) water
freshly ground black pepper
4 sprigs of basil, leaves picked

24 cm (9½ in) sauté pan

173

method

Put all the ingredients in the sauté pan and cook over a medium heat for about 25 minutes, stirring regularly. Serve immediately.

STIR-FRIED VERMICELLI WITH BROCCOLI

Preparation: 5 minutes
Cooking time: 8 minutes
Resting time: 10 minutes

Serves 4

200 g (7 oz) soya vermicelli
2 tablespoons olive oil
400 g (14 oz) broccoli, cut into florets
2 garlic cloves, chopped
30 g (1 oz) freshly grated ginger
1 teaspoon paprika
1 tablespoon sesame seeds

30 cm (12 in) frying pan (skillet)

method

Put the vermicelli in a large bowl of very hot water and allow to stand for
10 minutes. Heat the oil in the frying pan, add the broccoli florets, garlic,
ginger and paprika. Fry for 5 minutes, stirring. Drain the vermicelli and add to
the pan. Cook for a further 3 minutes, stirring.
Serve sprinkled with sesame seeds.

RICE SPAGHETTI WITH VEGETABLES

Preparation: 5 minutes
Cooking time: 25 minutes

176

Serves 4

200 g (7 oz) rice spaghetti
350 g (12 oz) white cabbage, shredded
2 leeks, rinsed and cut into fine strips
12 sprigs of coriander (cilantro), leaves picked
1 tablespoon curry powder
1 tablespoon nuoc mam (Vietnamese fish sauce)
200 ml (7 fl oz/scant 1 cup) coconut milk

750 ml (25 fl oz/3 cups) water
1 teaspoon salt

26 cm (10 in) casserole dish (Dutch oven)

method

Put all the ingredients in the casserole dish and cook over a medium heat for
about 25 minutes, stirring regularly. Serve with fresh coriander.

SOBA NOODLES WITH SWISS CHARD AND SHIITAKE MUSHROOMS

Preparation: 5 minutes
Cooking time: 20 minutes

178

Serves 4

200 g (7 oz) soba noodles
200 g (7 oz) Swiss chard, green part
   only, chopped
150 g (5 oz) chicken breast, cut into thin strips
150 g (5 oz) shiitake mushrooms, quartered
1 vegetable stock cube
1 tablespoon sesame oil
2 tablespoons soy sauce
1 litre (34 fl oz/4 cups) water

26 cm (10 in) frying pan (skillet)

method

Put all the ingredients in the frying pan and cook over a medium heat
for about 20 minutes, stirring regularly. Serve immediately.

DESSERTS

These delicately flavoured fruit parcels come with spices and even chocolate for a gentle end to your meal. They can also be enjoyed for breakfast or as a light snack.

APPLE PARCEL

Preparation: 5 minutes
Cooking time: 40 minutes

182

Serves 4

150 ml (5 fl oz) low-fat Greek yoghurt
4 apples, peeled
½ vanilla pod (bean), split and the seeds scraped out
1 tablespoon ground almonds (almond meal)
1 tablespoon honey

26 cm (10 in) casserole dish (Dutch oven) + steamer
  basket

method

Put 500 ml (17 fl oz/2 cups) of water in the casserole dish and add the
steamer basket. Put the yoghurt in the middle of a large sheet of baking
parchment, place the apples, vanilla pod and seeds on top, sprinkle with
ground almonds, drizzle with honey and fold over to make a parcel (or use
a cooking bag). Put in the casserole dish. Cover, bring to a boil and cook
over a low heat for 40 minutes. Open the parcel and serve hot or warm.

BANANA PARCEL

Preparation: 5 minutes
Cooking time: 20 minutes

Serves 4

100 ml (3½ fl oz/scant ½ cup)
   coconut milk
4 bananas, halved lengthways
4 squares of dark chocolate, grated

26 cm (10 in) casserole dish (Dutch oven)
   + steamer basket

method

Put 500 ml (17 fl oz/2 cups) of water in the casserole dish and add the
steamer basket. Pour the coconut milk into the middle of a large sheet of
baking parchment, add the bananas, sprinkle with grated chocolate and fold
over to make a parcel (or use a cooking bag). Put in the casserole dish.
Cover, bring to a boil and cook over a low heat for 20 minutes.
Open the parcel and serve hot or warm.

PEAR PARCEL

Preparation: 5 minutes
Cooking time: 20 minutes

Serves 4

3 pears, peeled and quartered
1 cinnamon stick
5 g (¼ oz) ginger, thinly sliced

24 cm (9½ in) saucepan + steamer basket

method

Put 500 ml (17 fl oz/2 cups) of water in the saucepan and add the steamer basket. Place all the ingredients on a large sheet of baking parchment and fold over to make a parcel (or use a cooking bag). Put in the saucepan. Cover, bring to a boil and cook over a low heat for 20 minutes.
Open the parcel and serve hot or warm.

PINEAPPLE PARCEL

Preparation: 5 minutes
Cooking time: 30 minutes

188

Serves 4

1 pineapple, peeled and cut into 1 cm (½ in) rounds
1 vanilla pod (bean), split and the seeds scraped out
1 star anise
2 tablespoons rum

24 cm (9½ in) saucepan + steamer basket

method

Put 500 ml (17 fl oz/2 cups) of water in the saucepan and add the steamer
basket. Place all the ingredients on a large sheet of baking parchment and
fold over to make a parcel (or use a cooking bag). Put in the saucepan.
Cover, bring to a boil and cook over a low heat for 30 minutes.
Open the parcel and serve immediately.

INDEX

+ TURKEY WITH CREAM AND MUSHROOMS **136**
+ PORK TENDERLOIN WITH WHITE CHICORY **126**
+ CHICKEN WITH BUTTERNUT SQUASH AND PISTACHIOS **108**
+ MUSHROOM RISOTTO **170**

MACKEREL
+ MACKEREL CASSEROLE **112**
+ MACKEREL PARCEL **86**

MANGETOUT PEAS
+ KING PRAWN PARCEL **88**
+ PAN-FRIED PRAWNS AND VEGETABLES **128**

MISO
+ SPINACH AND TOFU BROTH **50**

MONKFISH
+ MONKFISH BROTH **54**

MUSHROOM
+ KOMBU SEAWEED BROTH **64**
+ TURKEY WITH CREAM AND MUSHROOMS **136**
+ FUSILLI PASTA WITH MUSHROOMS **168**
+ VIANDE DES GRISONS (AIR-DRIED BEEF) OMELETTE **104**
+ PAN-FRIED CHICKEN LIVERS **124**
+ MUSHROOM RISOTTO **170**
+ RICE WITH VEAL AND MUSHROOMS **162**
+ MUSHROOM AND CHESTNUT VELOUTÉ SOUP **42**

MUSSELS
+ MUSSEL CASSEROLE **116**

OLIVES
+ MEDITERRANEAN VEGETABLE CASSEROLE **30**
+ TOMATO, OLIVE AND HERB OMELETTE **100**
+ SKATE, TOMATO AND OLIVE PARCEL **80**

ONION
+ MACKEREL CASSEROLE **112**
+ ONION SOUP **68**

ORANGE
+ STEAMED CARROT PARCEL **92**
+ SEA BASS PARCEL **78**

PARSNIP
+ VEGETABLE BOLOGNESE **36**
+ QUINOA, CARROTS AND PARSNIPS **144**
+ AUTUMN TAGLIATELLE **34**

PEAR
+ PEAR PARCEL **186**

PEAS
+ SPRING CASSEROLE **26**
+ SAUTÉED BEEF WITH PEAS **132**
+ VEGETABLE RISOTTO **172**

PEPPER
+ SUMMER CASSEROLE **28**
+ MEDITERRANEAN VEGETABLE CASSEROLE **30**
+ LENTILS WITH TOFU **146**
+ PAN-FRIED TURKEY WITH PEPPERS **106**
+ PAN-FRIED PEPPERS AND SWEETCORN WITH GOAT'S CHEESE **18**
+ PAN-FRIED TUNA AND VEGETABLES **134**
+ VEGETABLE RISOTTO **172**
+ BROWN RICE WITH VEGETABLES **164**

PINEAPPLE
+ PINEAPPLE PARCEL **188**
+ VEAL WITH PINEAPPLE **130**

PINE NUTS
+ STEAMED FRENCH BEAN PARCEL **96**

PISTACHIOS
+ STEAMED CARROT PARCEL **92**
+ CHICKEN WITH BUTTERNUT SQUASH AND PISTACHIOS **108**

PLANT-BASED CREAM
+ SALMON PARCEL **76**

PLANT-BASED DRINK
+ MUSHROOM AND CHESTNUT VELOUTÉ SOUP **42**

PORK
+ PORK TENDERLOIN WITH WHITE CHICORY **126**

POTATO
+ LENTILS WITH TOFU **146**

POTIMARRON SQUASH
+ CHICKEN, POTIMARRON SQUASH AND DATE CASSEROLE **114**

PRAWNS
+ PAN-FRIED PRAWNS AND VEGETABLES **128**
+ RICE NOODLES WITH PRAWNS **158**

QUARK
+ CHICKEN AND CELERIAC PARCEL **82**

QUINOA
+ QUINOA AND VEGETABLE CASSEROLE **154**
+ QUINOA, CARROTS AND PARSNIPS **144**

RABBIT
+ RABBIT WITH CARROTS **122**

RAISINS
+ BURGHUL WITH TOMATOES **142**
+ BROWN RICE WITH VEGETABLES **164**

RAVIOLI
+ RAVIOLI BROTH **62**

RED RADISH
+ PAN-FRIED PRAWNS AND VEGETABLES **128**

RICE
+ RICE WITH VEAL AND MUSHROOMS **162**
+ BROWN RICE WITH VEGETABLES **164**
+ RED RICE WITH CALAMARI **166**

RICE NOODLES
+ RICE NOODLES WITH PRAWNS **158**
+ RICE SPAGHETTI WITH VEGETABLES **176**

RISOTTO RICE
+ MUSHROOM RISOTTO **170**
+ VEGETABLE RISOTTO **172**

SALMON
+ SALMON PARCEL **76**

SCALLOPS
+ SCALLOP PARCEL **72**

SEA BASS
+ SEA BASS PARCEL **78**

SEAWEED
+ KOMBU SEAWEED BROTH **64**

SHORT PASTA
+ SWISS CHARD AND VERMICELLI BROTH **44**
+ CHICKEN AND VERMICELLI SOUP **46**
+ FUSILLI PASTA WITH MUSHROOMS **168**
+ STIR-FRIED VERMICELLI WITH BROCCOLI **174**

SKATE
+ SKATE, TOMATO AND OLIVE PARCEL **80**

SOBA NOODLES
+ KOMBU SEAWEED BROTH **64**
+ SOBA NOODLES WITH SWISS CHARD AND SHIITAKE MUSHROOMS **178**

SPINACH
+ SPINACH AND TOFU BROTH **50**
+ AUTUMN CASSEROLE **24**
+ BROCCOLI AND TOFU PARCEL **90**
+ SPINACH VELOUTÉ SOUP **48**

SWEETCORN
+ PAN-FRIED PEPPERS AND SWEETCORN WITH GOAT'S CHEESE **18**

SWEET POTATO
+ TURKEY WITH SWEET POTATOES AND SPICES **110**

SWISS CHARD
+ SWISS CHARD AND VERMICELLI BROTH **44**
+ SOBA NOODLES WITH SWISS CHARD AND SHIITAKE MUSHROOMS **178**

TOFU
+ CHILLI BROTH **66**
+ SPINACH AND TOFU BROTH **50**
+ LENTILS WITH TOFU **146**
+ BROCCOLI AND TOFU PARCEL **90**
+ COURGETTE AND TOFU VELOUTÉ SOUP **56**

TOMATO
+ VEGETABLE BOLOGNESE **36**
+ BURGHUL WITH TOMATOES **142**
+ CHICKPEA AND TOMATO CASSEROLE **148**
+ MEDITERRANEAN VEGETABLE CASSEROLE **30**
+ LENTIL AND HADDOCK CASSEROLE **152**
+ TOMATO, OLIVE AND HERB OMELETTE **100**
+ CHICKEN AND CELERIAC PARCEL **82**
+ SKATE, TOMATO AND OLIVE PARCEL **80**
+ SAUTÉED BEEF WITH PEAS **132**
+ RED RICE WITH CALAMARI **166**
+ SPAGHETTI WITH TOMATOES **160**

TUNA
+ PAN-FRIED TUNA AND VEGETABLES **134**

TURKEY
+ TURKEY WITH CREAM AND MUSHROOMS **136**
+ TURKEY WITH SWEET POTATOES AND SPICES **110**
+ TURKEY, LEEK AND COCONUT PARCEL **84**
+ PAN-FRIED TURKEY WITH PEPPERS **106**

TURNIP
+ SPRING CASSEROLE **26**

VANILLA POD
+ PINEAPPLE PARCEL **188**
+ APPLE PARCEL **182**

VEAL
+ RICE WITH VEAL AND MUSHROOMS **162**
+ VEAL WITH PINEAPPLE **130**

WHITE CHICORY
+ PORK TENDERLOIN WITH WHITE CHICORY **126**

WHITE WINE
+ MACKEREL CASSEROLE **112**
+ RABBIT WITH CARROTS **122**

This edition published in 2023 by Hardie Grant Books, an imprint of Hardie Grant Publishing.
First published in 2019 by Hachette Livre (Marabout), 2019.
Original title: Juste Une Casserole Light (ISBN 978-2-501-13908-3).
All rights reserved.

Hardie Grant Books (London)
5th & 6th Floors
52–54 Southwark Street
London SE1 1UN

Hardie Grant Books (Melbourne)
Building 1, 658 Church Street
Richmond, Victoria 3121
hardiegrantbooks.com

British Library Cataloguing-in-Publication Data. A catalogue
record for this book is available from the British Library.

One-Pot Healthy
ISBN: 978-1-78488-616-5

10 9 8 7 6 5 4 3 2

FOR MARABOUT
Proofreader: Emmanuel Caroux and Véronique Dussidour
Design: Chimène Denneulin

FOR HARDIE GRANT
Publishing Director: Kajal Mistry
Senior Project Editor: Chelsea Edwards
Proofreader: Caroline West
Translator: Alison Murray
Typesetter: David Meikle
Production Controller: Sabeena Atchia

Colour reproduction by p2d
Printed and bound in China by Leo Paper Products Ltd.